I Am
My
Own
Garden

SATINDER KAUR

I Am My Own Garden

Published by Made to Change the World™ Publishing
Nashville, Tennessee

Cover and interior designed by Chelsea Jewell

Paperback ISBN: 978-1-956837-39-1
Ebook ISBN: 978-1-956837-40-7

Printed in the USA, Canada, Australia, and Europe

Dedicated to those who, like me,
    have penned their thoughts in solitude
    crafting art yet to see the light.
As I finally unveil these verses
    may they serve as an invitation for you to do the same.
Your whispered melodies hold the essence of untold stories
    and your unspoken truths yearn to bloom within the
    pages of this world.

CONTENTS

Acknowledgments

In the following pages, you'll delve into the poetic journey of some seasons of my life. It's a journey nurtured by the love and aspirations of my parents, S. Gurdev Singh and Smt. Parkash Kaur, who, in their own ways, fanned the flames of creativity within me. Sometimes I ponder: What verses might have flowed from my father's pen had life's demands not intervened? What stories might my mother have told if the gates of education were open to her? Their dreams, though unvoiced, have become the tapestry of my own artistic path.

To my spiritual teacher, His Holiness Sri Sri Ravi Shankar, who has illuminated my way, offering wisdom, love, faith, and a profound way of living that lends meaning to my existence.

To my daughters, Alisha Grewal and Prisha Grewal, whose unwavering belief in my words has been the wind beneath my wings. I want them to have access to all the writings flowing through me so that they don't wonder as to what my soul must have been singing. I hope to be the living example of dreams fulfilled to show them that no ambition is too grand, no path too uncharted.

To my dear friends, whose appreciation and encouragement have been a constant source of support. Your belief in my poetry has provided me the courage to share my words, and your help has made the publication of this book possible.

Introduction

It was a beautiful summer day of my fifth grade in India, the country of my birth. I was enjoying the monsoon rain while looking at the light pink roses that I had planted. Though the wind and heavy rain lashed them, I felt the roses were smiling through it all. It was then, inspired by nature, that I wrote my first poem.

Since that moment during my childhood, I have been writing poetry. Sometimes in my journal, sometimes waking up in the middle of the night and scribbling on whatever piece of paper I find. Now the Notes app of my smartphone is mostly where I write.

For all these years, my verses remained hidden from the world's gaze as life's currents swept me along. It was amidst wreckage of what I once held dear that I found myself at a crossroad grappling with questions of identity and purpose. In the gentle guidance of my spiritual teacher, Sri Sri Ravi Shankar, I was able to weather life's storms, to find strength in vulnerability and courage in adversity.

And, through introspection and resilience, I found courage to unveil my poetry to the world. Through this book, I lay bare my journey of transformation, healing, and finding my own self.

I hope this book serves as a beacon of hope for anyone traveling through life's storms, a reminder that even the heaviest clouds pass and the sun shines once more. It's a gentle whisper to say that it's okay to lower your guard, to let the tears fall, and to let your vulnerability be your strength.

In the moments of despair, when it seems as though the world has turned its back, know that you are not alone. From the ashes of pain and the depths of despair, you will rise stronger, wiser, and more resilient. Your journey through the valleys will lead to the grandest peaks.

For those who find themselves on the spiritual path, a journey toward universal love and oneness, it can be a lonely road at times. It's not always easy to find kindred spirits who comprehend the profoundness of this journey. But, in the pages of this book, I hope you discover a companion, someone who walks with you in both the dazzling light of realization and the comforting shade of reflection. You are not alone in your pursuit of deeper understanding and connection with the divine.

We all journey on life's roller coaster through the highs and lows. Having someone who can resonate with both the brilliance and the shadows, someone who can make you feel seen, heard, understood, and not alone is a cherished gift. I hope that in these pages you find that gift.

Words end where truth begins

SECTION 1:

The boundless space

Invocation

Let every breath I take
    be used in service
Let every beat of my heart
    sing in devotion
Let there be peace
    in the inner and outer world
And let every life be
    an eternal celebration!!!!

Strength in love

Let love be your strength, not weakness
Let togetherness be your freedom, not bondage
Let smiles be your jewels, not diamonds
Let compassion be your guide, not anguish

In the embrace of your heart

There are moments
    when you want to
    take the whole world
    in the embrace of your heart
Love pours out
    from each cell
    of your being
    for no reason
It feels like
    there is no other
    but only deep stillness
    with your soul singing in devotion
So precious are those moments
    and your heart gets soaked
    in immense appreciation!!

Out of mind's reach

Time and again I realize
     that there is no one
     between me and my happiness
     except my own mind
This mind can keep me bounded
     or I can go beyond its reach
     living as freely and boundless
     as I am truly meant to be

Stillness so profound

As I sit in this room full of
    tables and chairs
My senses are heightened by
    sights and sounds that fill the air
Pots and wall decor adorn the space
    as a gentle breeze whispers with grace
The comfortable couch I sit on is white
Green plants on the tables
    bring a sense of life
Empty cups of tea, a wall clock ticking
Though no one is around, still there is something
My heart can feel it, but eyes can't see
    a oneness with surroundings and me
My body melts into the couch with ease
My mind expands and floats on the breeze
It's strange how everything seems to be
    a part of me yet separate from me
A little voice in my head suggests
    it's now time to
    switch off the lights and leave
But the peace and deep rest
    is too much to believe
The moment is here, and it's profound
My eyes are open, and words resound
Though I am not here, yet I am
I can sit here forever just like this

The clock's tick tock echoes
    through the air
    as I close my eyes and breathe in
    the stillness present there
Air moves through my skin
But nothing reaches the depth of stillness
    present within me and here

Longing in contentment

I am happy and content
    yet I am seeking
Quiet and present
    yet very intense is my longing
I feel you with me
    yet I am waiting

Tears of devotion

Tears of devotees are truly precious
Words alone cannot express their value
    as we share the stories of grace and love
Our words create a sacred silence with us
In this silence, each and everything in the world
    seems to be a part of us
Mind seems empty and heart full
Such a beautiful wonder takes over
And we come in touch with
    the essence of our true selves

Divinity within

Unpleasant dreams
  don't scare me
And pleasant ones
  don't allure me
There is this space
  inside me
  where all is well
  all is taken care of
Where love blossoms
  and faith shines
Living surrendered
  to that divinity inside me

Warmth of boundless space

Sitting inside my warm house
    while outside it's freezing cold
    my mind often wanders to
    a place beyond this physical realm
    where my soul would be free to roam
    when I am neither in this body
    nor in the comfort of this home
I ponder where I might exist
    once my time on this Earth is done
    and who I am at my very core
    beneath the layers that I've spun
Then I find solace in meditation
    for it reveals a boundless space
    where all questions fade away
    and stillness takes its place
In that peaceful state of being
    I touch the essence of my soul
Something tells me I will be alright
    no matter where time takes me
I will always be complete and whole

Intoxicated in divine love

I have nothing to prove or achieve
Just a deep sense of relaxation and ease
I'm at total comfort
        smiling for no reason
Divine love is such an intoxication
        and I am happily in it
I have no need to strive
        or seek validation
For I am content with
        where I am in this moment
Divine love is full of grace
        and I am happily in its pure elation

Springing into infinity

The spring under my feet
The song in my heart, so sweet
A smile on my lips and
    the twinkle in my eyes
    say only one thing: love
This love of the divine
    which never really dies
The love that connects us all
A presence ever so powerful
A blessed life that's ours to share
    on this beautiful day
    that's truly wonderful
The moment of eternity
    that I can feel so purely
    says only one thing:
That we are united in belonging
    like the circle of infinity

Blooming in love

When love blooms in the heart
    it brings a spring in the step
    a smile on the face
    and the whole world in its embrace
Today I feel something like this
    and I see you smiling within me
Our union is infinite
    and the entire universe dances in its glee

Flow of bliss

There is a deep longing
    in my heart
There is a blissful union
    in my being
Longing and union
    both side by side
    in sweet communion
Today it's a rain
    of bliss beyond the words
    a feeling that soars, like free birds
As this rain pours down
    a symphony of joy
    a heavenly sound
It drenches my being
    swells up my heart
    and flows to everyone around

Beyond the veil of time

Though no one has
    any control on you
    Oh almighty time,
Your ceaseless march
    is both relentless
    and boundless
Yet if it be your will
    I plead for a moment still
    to relish this precious delight
    to bask in love's sweet sight
For my dreamy desires
    have just now
    started waking up
The spring of my heart
    has just now
    started flowering up
The face of my beloved
    has just now
    come out of the veil
So, let me linger
    just a little more
    to cherish this bliss
    to my core
For in this moment
    so precious and rare
    I find my joy, love
    solace and loving care

Let me soak
    in this moment a little longer
Let me hold it
    in my heart forever
Before you move on
    and this moment goes by
    into the past forever

Eternal connection

A presence I have felt
    for as long as I can remember
    amidst the chaos of life's pace
I didn't know what it was
    but it held me in its embrace
    like the blanket of grace
    though it had no face
For years I wondered
    if I would ever know
    what this presence truly was
    to what I had surrendered
Up until I met you in person
    the familiarity was my reason
    that this presence, this beacon
    was none other than you
With that comforting connection
    my soul had this instant recognition
    and my senses tuned into that observation
My heart joyfully found this reassurance
    of my being forever be in your presence
And it will forever be my guide
    always present right by my side
    no matter where I go, what I do
It will cheer me on with graceful sight
    walking me through darkness and light

Longing's journey

Moonlight shines bright, tonight
    as I travel in my heart
    to where you are, my heart's delight
Tall trees, moonlit sky
    glowing faces, sparkling eyes
    joyful beings soaring high
Around you is all fun, bliss, and divine
I travel to the moon
    become the soft glow of its light
My radiance enters through a window
    falling on your lotus feet, gratitude in sight
Tonight, I am the moon, the trees
    the travel, the light
    once again, content in my longing
Tonight, I am the longing

Basking in the moment

Today seems happier
    lighter, brighter
My heart seems to
    be bigger, lovelier
It's first day of summer
    or the anticipation of Sri Sri's
    arrival in the US
Whatever the reason may be
    it's bringing happiness within me
My soul sings delightfully
    my heart dances joyfully
A big smile shining on my face
    the world seems to be in my embrace
I am letting my mind out of the way
    I am getting my heart only to say
As I bask in this moment
    which feels like a present
I am thanking, appreciating
    celebrating and rejoicing

Could, would, should

Just being
In this moment
In this space
Letting go of what was
Could be, would be, or should be
Just being
In this moment
Accepting it for
        what it is
Not wishing for
        it to be any other way
Words are so shallow
Silence is too deep
        in this moment
It's boundless, it just is
I embody the silence
The space
The moment
The essence I am

From my heart to the universe

My heart seems
    to be overflowing with love
Like a cloud which can't
    contain the water anymore
So, it bursts to
    showering the Earth
Today you can expect
    the rain to fall
Rain of grace and bliss
Rain of love and light
For the entire universe
    to get soaked in it

Journeying with joy

    like the glow of a candle
    fragrance of a rose
    laughter of little babies
    and like a river flows
That's how I am feeling
A smile on my lips
A song in my heart
    like a fluffy white cloud
    gently passing by
    in the clear blue sky
That's how I am walking
    on this path called life

Eternal presence

Why am I so happy?
What is this fleeting feeling in my heart?
Where are the tears of joy coming from?
What is making me jumpy?
I cannot see or hear it
     I cannot touch or smell it
But I feel it, I feel it flowing in me
     I feel it in every cell
I feel it in every place I visit
     in every face that I look at
I sense its presence,
     so deep and so vast
     its stillness, its peace, its bliss
It's here, it's now and
     it's flowing to me in me

Ocean of promise

I am the ocean of love and the presence
    in this moment; I am all that you are seeking
Look no further, go nowhere, do nothing
    for I am here ever loving and affirming
You are total, you are complete
    in this moment, the way you are
I am this moment, the time and beyond time
I am the ebb and flow of the cosmic tide
    the unwavering wave and the still ocean wide
I am the light of the sun, moon, and stars,
    the vast expanse of space
    and the Earth that births
I am all that there is
    Who is this giving these words?
    Who is this listening with awe?
    Who is this reading these words?
That is me, that is you
    and that's what there is, all is in it, and it is in all
I am that all and all is me, just me

SECTION 2:

Rooted in eternal bonds

Magical reflection

My daughters are laying under
　　the star-filled night sky
As I sit next to them
　　my heart in gratitude soars high
Soft cool breeze, happy faces
　　beautiful music filling the spaces
As we wait for the fireworks
　　and Disney's show to begin
This land of dreams is becoming
　　even more magical herein
There are thousands of people around
　　no more spots left on the ground
Some are just sitting, waiting, talking
　　others walking by or eating
As my eyes are watching all this
　　my mind is slipping into quiet bliss
As peace and serenity washes over me
　　gratitude makes me feel so free
Everything is here yet not here
　　it's this moment, nothing out there
Stillness of water reflecting the castle
　　and stillness of mind reflecting the self

Retreat rejoice

One whole year of playing different roles
    to the best of my abilities
Now it's time to leave it all
    and come to you, oh divine entity
Though it's only for a few days
    but those days are my infinity
Let me rejoice in your presence
    let me celebrate my being
I can hardly wait
    for the moments to start
For the time to slow down
    and life's rhythms to impart
    wings to my feet and
    a song to my heart
As I head to the meditation retreat with Sri Sri, I depart

Breath's infinite sway

Did you gently slip into the chambers of my heart
    as I got into the rhythms of my breath
        doing kriya today?
For I felt love gushing through the doors of my core
    deep longing made me cry in bliss
I journeyed beyond the seven skies
    where all I could hear was my soul's singing
        the song of devotion and love it was bringing
My breath, not my own, carried me away
    sweeping me off my mind
        in love's infinite sway
My being merged with the universe
    and all burdens were taken away
What a blessing to just sit and breathe
    and come out with a heart
        full of gratitude
For me, every day is Teacher's day
    every day a thanksgiving
For as long as
    tears of longing wash my face
        taking me to soul's boundless space
Thank you Sri Sri for guiding me to light
With your wisdom, my being shines so bright

Divinity listens

Talking to you is like breathing air
    so effortless and natural
It never fails to amaze me
    how you listen every time, everywhere
In your presence, I feel no fear
    everything becomes crystal clear
When I look at your twinkling eyes
    through my moist eyes
They seem to be smiling even more
    and make me smile a lot more
I know you hear me in silence
    even what is left unspoken
Though sometimes I forget this
    but my heart remains awoken
My botherations get dropped
    dreams, desires get surrendered
I exist in you, trust in you
    and pray someday soon
    this duality disappears, too
Till then, I talk to you
    and that's all I do
Sometimes in words, others in silent prayer
    and you listen every time, everywhere

Blessed inspiration

Some years back
    in a moment of eternity
    you walked towards me
As I stood in total wonder
    I felt the universe
    moving towards me
You placed your blessings-filled
    hand on my head
    saying, "Yes, she will do
    and she will do a lot more"
I put my head on your shoulder
    not knowing what you meant
But it was a moment
    of unsaid, unseen,
    unheard of wonder, of bliss
As I spaced out
    or I dissolved into nothingness
    I felt as if there was no me
    there was no you
If there was anything
    it was just this nothingness
    a nothingness of pure joy
    utmost peace, of wonder
Do I even have words to say
    what it was?
It took me time to realize
    what you meant
    what a huge blessing it was

and then miracles happened
Including mine, thousands of
    lives were transformed
Somewhere down the road
    I forgot this nothingness
    this purpose of my soul
But today again
    a day after Guru Purnima
    I remember it all
I remember that moment
    all those moments
    when you kindled
    my soul in so many ways
Time and again, you
    picked me up like
    a delicate rose
"Yes Guruji," I will do
    I will do a lot more
Just the way
    you said it
Just the way
    you travel place to place
Just the way you
    unite heart to heart
I will do it, too
It may still be like
    a drop in the ocean
    but I will carry

the fragrance of your love
and knowledge forward
For this is
my life's goal
For this is the calling
of my soul

Have you arrived?

I want to leave behind everything
    and go, run, fly on the happy wings
    of my longing
Through the clouds
    over the mountains
Swimming through
    the sea of emotions
Whatever comes my way
    I will take it like flowers
I want to pick a rose
    for you on the way
What if you are waiting
    for me when I arrive
And you say, "Hmm, you have arrived?
    How was your trip? Are you happy now?"
I would then be speechless as usual
    just smiling cheek to cheek
    and say, "Yes Guruji!"
I am sitting here in my home
    scrolling through my friends' posts
    to see if someone has posted
    any pictures of you arriving in DC
In my heart
    I can hear the giggles, the laughter
    the hustling sound of their feet
    walking fast, running behind you
I can feel the stillness
    of their minds

and the joy of their hearts
It makes me cry happy tears
    as my smile shines through my eyes
I wonder why I miss you so much?
    What it is in you that pulls me so much?
    Why do I feel content even in my longing?
I feel your presence, your love, your grace
    and, for now, I am rejoicing in my longing

A wish for lifetimes

Last year on my birthday
    I was blessed with a wish come true
You were here in the US
My birthday wish was
    to meet you in person
To celebrate my being
    in your presence
And it happened
    in the city of angels
    where I felt I was reborn
As I think back on those moments today
    I ask myself how this year do
    I want to celebrate my birthday
No desire comes to mind, except one
To meet you in a new way
    so there remains no separation
Like the river merges
    into the ocean
Like the sunlight comes
    from the sun
Like the fragrance blooms
    in the flowers
Let me find myself forever
    residing in your divine presence
Let my mind be centered and clear
Let my intellect be sharpened
Let my ego dissolve
Let me see you

everywhere my sight goes
May I live from the space
        where you reside
Let me realize the
        truth of life and beyond
This year, let me start
        walking in your footsteps
        step by step
        moment by moment
For times to come

Longing is a gift

In every pair of eyes, I see your twinkling smile
I feel your presence in the early morning sun
    peeking through my window
In the sweetness of the moon
    I find your loving care
The clouds, the sky, the water
    the earth, the trees are nothing
    but your sweet presence reflecting
Your essence is in every breeze
    igniting a spark within me
A smile so precious on my face
    a song in my heart of your grace
I am using so many words
    but these can hardly express
    what it is to feel your presence
        in every moment
        in every person
        in every situation
Sometimes a tear escapes
    and my throat chokes
    in intense gratitude and longing
Realizing what a precious gift
    it is to have this blessing
    making my life truly worth living

Sweet pain of longing

The sweet pain of longing
    grew stronger in my heart
When tears started rolling
    I found a prayer in my heart
As I was silently looking
    towards the sky up and above
In that moment I realized
    what love truly is, perhaps
"Oh infinite
    and splendid universe,
Please show me
    the next step and all others after
    those that lead me to you
    and bring you to me"
A smile filled me in that instant
    as I realized how
    alive I was in that moment
    in it being fully present
    embracing it without being resistant
Then a voice from deep inside said,

"Seek no further
as I am in you
as you are in me
we were never separated
and will never be apart
so just enjoy the journey
of sweet longing and learning
until our union becomes
a celebration in your own knowing"

Divine reminders

With the innocence of a child
    we seek answers from you, the wise one
Sometimes repeatedly the same question
    we ask like a stubborn one
But you, like a loving parent
    answer us every time
With patience and understanding
    every place, all the time
There are times when
    you don't say anything
Leaving us in wonder
    as to what is happening
Then, out of the blue, something shifts
    some event, some conversation
    a rainbow, a hollow emptiness
The curtain of confusion finally lifts
    we find our answer, the mind settles
Agitation vanishes, clarity comes
    passion returns and a force within awakens
We are reminded of our magnanimity
    and we are ready to conquer the world
It's a wonder how we keep forgetting
    and how gently you keep reminding
    over and over, again and again

The light of our Earth

Which words can describe
    the deep gratitude in my heart
What gestures can express
    the magnitude of your kind heart
How can I even imagine the abundance
    that entered my life with your presence
Your love, your grace, your wisdom so profound
    all the beauty in this world, in you I found
Your smile, your charisma, your every move
    all radiate the divine, the purest of truth
As the sun rises and sets in the sky
    your presence is felt by those who try
To grasp the magnitude of your being
    to feel the essence of what you are giving
Like the moonlight on the lotus in still waters
    you kindle in me peace now and forever
The blanket of your love gives me warmth
    when I shiver with my doubts and fears
Showers of your compassion keep me cool
    when I forget who I am and shed those tears
You are the beginning, the journey, and the end
    in you my dear Guruji, I have found a friend
I thank the universe for bringing you here
    and for blessing us all with your presence, so dear
On this special day, we celebrate your birth
    in all true ways, you are the light of our Earth

Grateful for dad's legacy

Another sun sets on another Father's Day
    but my gratitude for you is everyday
My dearest Papa in heaven
    I am grateful to the universe for letting me
    in this lifetime be your daughter
Wherever you are, I hope you
    still are proud of me
    as you always were
I hope I can carry forward
    your legacy of humanity, humility
    divinity and faith in the almighty
You showed me the path of honesty
    hard work and to live with simplicity
The values you instilled in me
    are like my guiding light
Keeping me grounded
    and my path to be bright

Miracle of my life

I am because of you
    and I love you
Happy birthday, my dearest daughter
Your arrival was a blessing
    a miracle divine
    a moment that changed
    my life forever
A joy to call you mine
You filled my heart with love
    and my days with laughter
An answer to my prayer
    that I'll cherish forever
Today, on your special day,
    this is what I wish to say
That you are the sunshine
    even on a rainy day
A pillar of my strength
    in your own gentle way
You are the reason
    for life's celebration
In you I see
    true love's own reflection
May the divine keep you smiling
    may you keep growing and glowing
Shining like the brightest star
    inspiring everyone near and far

Shining bright, a birthday ode to my daughter

Happy birthday to my first born
    my soul child, a daughter
    who is wiser than the wisest
    brighter than the brightest
Like a star in the sky
    my sunshine, "Alisha"
She is my friend and my companion
Indeed, a kind leader
    who dares to speak the truth
    even when it's hard to hear
With love and grace, she delivers
    the deepest life lessons
    so crystal clear
She is like my heartbeat
    that never stops
Standing by me
    like a tall, strong tree
    in the moments when
    I truly need someone
She is there
    just to be with me
Who knows how
    to live life in the moment
    with love and care
    with faith and devotion
Happy 14th birthday, my "Lado"
May each day ahead be joyful and fruitful

May you soar high in open skies
    and no ceiling can ever limit your flight
No matter where life takes you, my dear
    I'll be always support you and be there
Happy birthday, my beloved daughter!

Celebrating life's gift

As the clock ticks closer to midnight
    my heart beats faster in anticipation
For the day God blessed us with you
    to begin, the day of your birth
    and for the celebrations to begin
I remember it like it was yesterday
    the rush of emotions
    as you came into this world
Then you filled my days
    with joy, laughter, and cuteness
In you, Alisha found a sister
    and a forever best friend
Now, on your special day,
    I can't help but feel proud
    of the independent, confident
    and beautiful young girl
    you have become
With your keen observation
    with boldness and sense of direction
I thank God for blessing me
    with such a precious gift
And I pray for your happiness
    and success in all that you do
For you to shine like the sun
    be radiant like the full moon
As tears of gratitude roll
    down my cheeks

I smile through them
　　with a sense of knowingness
That I have raised you and
　　your sister well
And you both are under the
　　divine's love and support
On this day, I celebrate your life
　　your love and your growth
And I am honored to be your mother
Happy birthday, my precious Prisha

Déjà vu

As I close my eyes, memories flood my mind
    of a land that I left but can never leave behind
I feel the spring in my hair
I can smell the dewy grass under my feet
    and the scent of roses in the garden that used to grow
I hear the chirping of the birds and
    the temple bells ringing near
At a little distance the chanting of "homas"
    that I still hold dear
    and burning of holy fire
    the sight of a riverbank, a boat
    and the flowing water
    takes me back to a time
    of innocence and laughter
Kids playing barefoot on the softest of dust
    the clouds, the falling raindrops
    and the Earth's sweet smell
    the umbrella of a big tree, the nearby tea stand
    a boy with tea glasses, the dripping water
    and warmth of tea and land's affection
Sky meets the Earth, water flows to rivers
    and rivers to the sea
A cycle of nature that always
    fills me with glee

It all merges, it all flows
　　it all pauses for a moment
　　and then it continues, season is different
　　so is the place, the people and everything else
But is it really? different? or just the same

Seeds of faith

I am happy, living life to the fullest
Divine energy surges through me
     like a river in full flight
I see beauty in everything I see
I feel the presence in every
     moment of my life
On this Father's Day, I am offering
     my gratitude to you, again
As tears are rolling down my face
     tears of joy and intense
     longing for the divine
Papa, though you left this world
     the seeds of faith you sowed in me
     led me to dear Guruji
     who loves me more than
     it could ever be
I see you in him
     I feel you in him
     in every word and every deed
He fills my heart
     with love and bliss
     a love I never knew I'd need
On this Father's Day
I make a promise to you both
     that I will live my life
     spreading happiness
     to everyone crossing my path
     and keep striving to live

with unconditional happiness
For I am a reflection of you both

Ambrosia of my life

What can I say about you, my dear Mother?
    anything I say will be less
Even if I bring for you all the stars
    and all the flowers growing on Earth
Still, it will be far less
    for the precious life you have given to me
I hear your sweet voice ringing in my ears
    as you go about your chores, saying your prayers
    our happiness and health always in your prayers
My faith in the divine is your gift to me
Unconditional love only you showed to me
You carried me in your heart
    no matter where I went
    and stood by me in all life's events
I saw you getting shattered only
    when heavens took our father away
But then you took us under your wings
    and with all might carried on each day
You stood by us like a solid tree
    no matter how many storms we weathered
In your embrace we were safe and free
Soothing gentle presence of yours
    is like the ambrosia of my life
My heart smiles with your laughter
    and your wisdom lights my life
I feel so blessed to be your daughter
    celebrating this Mother's Day together

I wish for you to find the ultimate truth
    that you are seeking in this life
May we walk together for long
    in the future and in this life
May your prayer like life be an inspiration
    for now and for the next generation

A summer job

I used to ask you, "Papa,
    can I do a summer job?"
And you would answer, "Why?
    How much money do you need?"
"It's not about money, Papa,"
    I would insist, and you would
    lovingly say, "You work hard for studies
    you take it easy now, just help your mom."
Sometimes now, I wonder what would you say
    if you were still alive in the worldly sense
    seeing me working so hard, so long
What would you say, I wonder!!

The silence of mom's embrace

As Mom was departing for India
    at the airport, a bittersweet place
We had a longer, silent hug
    but it conveyed so much
    through those unsaid words
It kindled something deeper
    brought tears to my eyes
    and they kept rolling
    even after her flight took off
It made me realize
    how sweet and strong
    her presence in my life is
And no matter what life
    has brought our way
She always just prays
    for everyone's happiness
    for sorrows to vanish away
She is someone who knows
    how to truly be a giver
    whose love never withers away
For her divisions don't exist
    but oneness gets stronger every day
No wonder that I am her daughter
    a bond that surpasses any other

Father's eternal bond

As I gazed up at the limitless sky
    spread over Earth so wide and high
A soft breeze gently brushed my hair
    just like the way you used to care
Tears welled up from deep inside
    and washed my face with their tide
My heart felt shattered, cracked wide
You've been gone for a long time
But somehow, it feels you are here
    by my side, always near
How lucky I am to feel
    this pain of separation
Yet love blooms in my heart
    like an eternal celebration
Happy Father's Day, dear Dad!!!!

Cherishing family moments

Living every moment
    to the fullest
    when I am with
    my daughters
Being aware that
    time's tide is fastest
Some days just listening
    to their giggles
    while they play
    with their cousins
    all of them just chilling
As I make
    their favorite food
    and also watch them
    with a smile of gratitude
Before the busyness takes hold
    I savor every moment
    as if it were made of gold
Our lives are intertwined
    through lifetimes old and new
    and whether near or far apart
Our bond remains forever true

Love's guiding visits

Long after they depart from sight
Sometimes their memory
    can overwhelm you with might
Intense longing fills the heart and eyes
In those moments of deep despair
    you wonder if they're truly there
    visiting you to offer their love
    and guide you from above
To make sure you remain strong
    that you don't lose trust in love
    and in kindness
Have you ever felt like this?
Like I am feeling it
    diving in it
    and wondering if love truly is
    beyond time and space?
Especially the love of a father
Miss you Dad!!!

Loyal and selfless companion

Amidst the hustle and bustle of daily life
A faithful friend awaits me at the door
    his eager eyes gleaming with pure delight
    and he greets me with the same joy each time
Regardless of how long I've been gone
    he just showers me with all his love
    and waits patiently for our usual walk time
Our walks together are an enchanting escape
    the world is ours to explore and shape
Though together we both let each other be
    and enjoy each other's company in silence
All along the way he goes on sniffing
Usually this late out there no one else is walking
But we breathe in the cool breeze
    admiring the beautiful city views
    and some stars in the sky twinkling
Now and then I do tell him
    that he is loved, and he is amazing
As he looks back at me lovingly
    I know he is listening and understanding
    and I find my heart thanking and smiling
Symbol of unconditional love
    Buddy is a true companion

SECTION 3:

Phases of the full moon

The sun will shine again

The sun will shine brightly
    after the darkest night
As no clouds can long
    obscure its healing light
Whether it's rain, storm
    or fiercest of hail
Love is eternal
    and it will never fail
Life is a journey
    with ups and downs to show
But hope and faith
    make it a beautiful flow
It knows how to bounce back
    sooner than we know

Harmony of duality

Can you perceive the shimmering light
    that glows within the deepest night?
Can you hear the gentle hush
    that whispers in the loudest rush?
Can you grasp the boundless space
    that stretches to infinity's grace?
Can you fathom the serene stillness
    that exists amid all busyness?
Can you recognize the hidden darkness
    that permeates even the brightest brightness?
Can you discern the subtle movement
    that resides in the most tranquil moment?

Steps of determination

When you take the step
    towards your mission
    towards the purpose of your life
Be unstoppable and steady
But don't be afraid to adjust
    when the path ahead
    seems unsteady
Go with total commitment
    and don't quit when
    faced with adversity
Especially when that step is
    towards the betterment of the world
    towards the happiness of others
The journey may not
    always be easy
But faith in your heart
    courage in your steps
    determination in your mind and
    intensity in each pore
    will make you
    overcome any obstacles
    and make even the thorns
    seem like soft petals

Heaven within us

The way to heaven lies
    within our own hearts
The heart is the temple
    where divinity resides
It's the doorway to a world
    where love and peace coincide
If we listen closely
    we can hear the soft whispers
    of our soul guiding us
    towards the eternal lighthouse
On this journey, we must shed
    our cravings and aversions
    leaving behind all doubts
    and letting go of all expectations
So, let's take a moment
    to look within our hearts
    and uncover the heaven
    that's always been present within
The way to heaven indeed
    lies within our being
    and it's up to us to unleash
    the infinite that's all pervading

Magic of reality

We are our own reality
    creating it every moment
By connecting with
    ourselves in stillness
Where we access a space
    of true fulfillment
The universe which then unfolds
    is our own destiny
Shaped by our thoughts
    and inner clarity
Just closing our eyes, sitting, meditating
    and experiencing the magic unfolding

Patience

What to do when
    things move at snail's pace
    and you are ready to soar
    like a falcon in the race
Patience is the refuge
    you must embrace
For it'll help you
    maintain a steady pace
Be flexible, make
    adjustments as needed
But don't let your spirit
    ever be defeated

Student for life

Be a student now and always
Wisdom can come to you
        in so many ways
When you are eager to learn
        at every corner and turn
        your mind will expand
        and humility will dawn
        in your life in return

Faith brings grace

A devotee may falter
    but will never drown
For their faith will
    lift them from depth profound
And when the fog clears
    a new path is found
    leading them upward
    to bliss unbound
Then they realize that
    descent to the ocean's floor
    revealed depth and truth
    never seen before
With faith comes grace
    making them stronger
    than before

Hollow and empty

Very fortunate are those
    who can experience
    the hollow, empty space of mind
Where all that's needed
    is to simply be
Where the prayers come from
    a selfless place
    wishing happiness for all
Where distances dissolve
    with the magic of grace
Blessed to know
    many who walk this path
    and feel the presence
    of something beyond
    something deep and profound
As if it is just part of us
    it is being within us
    and a voice whispers,
    "You and I are just One.
    Together, we make the presence."

Healing breath

Distorted emotions can be
    like a heavy rock
    on our delicate heart
Through stillness and calmness
    we can find our way
    to melt away the pain
    that keeps us at bay
Our breath becomes our guide, our light
    and with each breath, we can banish the night
The power of meditation, it's clear to see
    is a path to love and inner harmony
    and though it's not the only way
    it can be a beacon on a darkened day
So, let us deep breathe, let us meditate
    to find our balance and to navigate
    the choppy waters of life's unknown
    with a heart full of love and
    seeds of hope sown

Love as love

Love beyond reasons
    expectations and relations
    pure and unfettered
    an eternal elation
Love just as love
    when it fills your heart
    you soar up high
    your smile shines bright
    like the sun in the sky
Life blooms anew
    with each passing day
    impacting everything
    that comes its way
It happens when
    you surrender to the divinity
    you move towards humanity
    and let love guide you
    with focus on infinity
When your inner self
    you cherish and adore
    and see the same in everyone
    in the world you explore

Service serves

When you put your hundred percent
    towards bringing some relief
    to people around you
Giving selflessly and
    surrendering the outcome
It can bring profound peace
    that emanates from within
Impacting not only oneself
    but also those around us
Evoking tears of gratitude
    and happiness appears within us

What is home

Buildings are not homes
    and homes are not forever
    they change, too
Sometimes, home could be a place
    sometimes, just a moment in time
    a look, a laugh, a silence, a sound
Any time, any place when we feel
    completely comfortable, content
That is home, sweet like bliss!

Words and vibes

As we wish someone well on their special day
Let's pause and check our own state of mind
We may find that we are not so happy and bright
But that's alright
Let's focus on our own inner light
    take a moment to appreciate
    the gifts we've received
    nature's abundance and
    blessings we've achieved
Let gratitude fill us up and
    bring a smile to our face
Then share that happiness
    with love and grace
And if we are already
    feeling joyous and content
Let our words and actions
    be heartfelt and sent
So that others can feel
    the good vibes we impart
    and our smiles can light up
    the world and each heart

Be the sunshine

In the snowy weather
     be the sunshine to someone
Give them the warmth of your love and smile
     and see the universe pouring blessings on you
Soak it all in and meditate
     and soon in glory you will be singing
...I am the sunshine!!!

Being centered

Situations come
     to throw you off balance
But just remembering
     who you are
Beyond your body, thoughts
     and emotions
May help you be centered!!

Flow like a river

Some will walk with you
	for a little while
Some may try
	to even put you down
But you must stay true
	to your path, your purpose
	and dreams that you've found
Your heart has courage
	and your feet bear unbreakable strength
So, you keep going until
	you reach the ultimate length
Just like water
	which does not stop
	for anything
It may pause
	and slow down at times
	but it goes on
	until it merges
	into the ocean

The voice within

Listen to a voice calling
    from deep within you
It knows you better
    than you do
    and it is whispering
    what path is meant for you
That path may not be the easiest
    or most obvious one
But it's the one that will make
    your life a meaningful one
So, follow that voice, my dear
    and let it guide you
    through every twist and turn
For it knows the steps towards
    a life of purpose and fulfillment

Phases of the full moon

As they gaze at the glory of the full moon
    many admire its fullness
But who considers
    the becoming of the full moon?
The journey it goes through
    in different phases and stages
    it still shines on
    with untiring spirit
    it constantly carries on
In the perception of the world
    it comes and goes
    it seems incomplete or whole
But does it ever cease to be what it is?
You, too, are like the moon
    sometimes feeling incomplete
    yet always perfect as you are
It's okay sometimes to feel
    whatever you need to heal
As feelings don't define you
    nor what you do or don't do
You remain what you truly are
    through the ups and downs
Different emotion, comes and goes
    but the essence of you, forever flows
So, take a moment tonight
    sit under the open sky
Watch the moon
    and reflect on who you truly are

You will soon be witnessing
    the darkness dissolving
    peace dawning and your energy uplifting
    a wonder inside you awakening
    and any moment may turn into
    the full moon's becoming

The world of silence

Silence is a world beyond the words
    a realm that can only be felt
It transcends all that we know
    and every emotion we have felt
In its space, there is serenity
    and nothing in this world
    can describe it's eternity

Play fully

There is no victory or defeat
    it's all only in the mind
    so just play full out
What matters is how you play
    and not what happens in the end
Ending and beginning is,
    again, only in the mind!!!

The veil lifted

The veil of illusion
        can seem impenetrable
        clouding the vision
        obscuring what's feasible
But, sooner or later,
        with trust in grace
        it does get lifted
        as nothing remains forever
Till then, be patient
        be gentle on yourself
Just remember that
        you will again
        shine bright
        in the mirror of sublime
        self's light
You will see the truth and
        everything will be alright

What if?

What if we could let go of
    the pressure to measure up
    to society's standards and norms
    of what success should look like
Instead, focus on our own journey
    and the unique path we are on
What if we define success
    as the progress we make
    while celebrating each small win
    each small step we take
Without judging ourselves
    as failures or successes
Breaking free from
    the chains of comparison
    and discovering the true meaning
    of success on our own terms
    at our own pace
    in our own time
    and in our own way
What if?

Transient existence

You, me, and all of us will vanish away
As no one remains forever
    though we are the eternity
Dust is all this body will turn into
    everything gone, nothing to hold on to
You are living as though you have forever
    but time is short, and death is very clever
Take a moment and ponder your worth
    and cherish every moment on this Earth
For the money in banks and relations we keep
    shall not go with us as we lay in final sleep
We came empty-handed and shall leave the same
    So why constantly be in the race for material gain?
Take some time in the solitude of your soul
    for it is what's constant and it keeps us whole

The perfect moment

Waiting for the perfect moment
    life can become miserable
Living every moment fully
    may bring perfection
    but if it doesn't
    then just let it be
Go out and make it happen
    and embrace every moment
    as it comes
Life is a precious gift
    meant to be lived fully each day
So, in your wait for the perfect moment,
    don't let your life slip away

The inexpressible

A picture may convey a lot
    they say a thousand words or not
    still, it has its limits
For how do you portray the stillness
    hollowness and infinity?
How do you show the state of beingness?
What images, what style can one employ
    to express this feeling, this endless joy
    beyond feelings, beyond gratitude
    beyond expression, this state of magnitude
Vast like the limitless sky!

Fill your cup

Be a giver, give
Be committed, recommit as and when needed
But, in this cycle, you must not forget
    that your own body and mind
    also need your care and rest
So, keep a little piece for yourself
    to elevate your happiness and peace
    so tomorrow there is no regret
For only what you have is
    what you can give
So, let this be the essence of your goal
    to fill your cup, to make yourself whole
    to serve with love from your abundance
    and share with others your radiance

Journey to miracles

Miracles don't just happen
      nor do they come from above
Instead, they reside within us
      in the depths of our soul
      in the form of divine love
But to witness such wonders
      we must dig deep within
      with unwavering faith to ponder
      and relentless journey to begin
      again and again

Rays of hope

No matter how dense the fog is
    the sun still finds a way to filter through
Its rays of light when shining bright
    bring us hope and dissolve away the night
Day after day, it comes to remind us
    that no matter how dark the clouds are
    the light of our being is sure to find us
So, hold on to those rays of hope
    and let them guide you, they sure got us

Happiness is your own inner light

Happiness is not a prize you win
    neither a struggle nor a competition
It is not a ball you chase around
    or a treasure that must be found
Instead, it waits for you
    to let go of the chase
    becoming still
    giving yourself some grace
    and there you find it
    in its rightful place
It was there all along
    inside your heart's glowing space
Like the sun that shines so bright
    happiness is your own inner light

Catalyst of celebration

What you see is just an illusion
What you don't see is the solution
     for your life to be a dance
     a celebration

SECTION 4:

For seasons beyond seasons

Cast in stone

In life we tend to judge and assume
    thinking we know what others should do
But who are we to judge and condemn
    when we don't even know exactly
    what they are going through?
We often think that we're invincible
    that nothing could ever go wrong
But life can be unpredictable
    and hardships can come along
The ones we judge may never have thought
    they'd face the trials they're going through
So, let's not be quick to pass a judgment
    but be compassionate and be present
For in this life, we never know
    when karma may laugh and show
So, let's be kind and empathetic
    and think before we cast in stone
For we may face a similar predicament
    and wouldn't want to face it alone

Uplifted

What can you give to anyone
  if you yourself are hurting?
How good is your company
  if you yourself are feeling lonely?
In some moments, this chatter
  in your mind can lead you
  into depths of sorrow, grief, and need
Watch out for it and shake it off
  like you shake off the dust from your clothes
  and remember that pain
  is not a lasting state
  and joy is waiting at the inner gate
You need only let the storm pass by
  and trust that joyful time is just nearby
Also remember to share your gifts
  and give what you can, despite your struggles
For in lifting others, you may find
  that you lift yourself, too, overcoming your hurdles

Testing times

In life there come times
　　when you feel like you're being tested
Shaken to your very core
　　again and again
It's up to you to fall defeated
　　or rise stronger and unbroken
Life brings us times
　　when our choice can make us
　　or break us
It's not what happens to us
　　but our response to the happenings
　　that matters the most
For it defines us and shapes our lives
　　and helps us remember lessons and learnings
　　that matter the most
So, what would you like to write
　　in the next chapter of your life?
How would you like
　　yourself to be described?
For the past is gone, and everything in it has vanished
Now you have a blank canvas of life
　　to paint with fresh perspective renewed
What do you want your future to hold?
　　That's the answer you need to find
For every time you fall or fail
　　it will help you win over your own mind

Lighten up

Lighten up my dear, lighten up
    let your spirit soar, dear one
    let it rise above the worries
    that cloud your skies
For life may be hard
    but you are strong
    and the trials you face
    won't last that long
Step outside and look
    up towards the sky
Feel the blessings
    coming from up high
Listen to the breeze
    as it gently sings
A melody of life
    that forever rings
Know that you are
    the center of this universe
A radiant light with a
    brilliance that can't be suppressed
Everything and everyone
    is here for you
    to support, to uplift
    to see you through
You are loved
    you are cherished
    and you are unique
    in every way

You—that is manifesting in you
    and in everything else
So, close your eyes and
    feel it in your heart
    the pulsating love
    which is your own part
    breathing through you
    smiling through you
Lighten up my dear, lighten up
    and let it show
For the world is waiting
    to see you glow
    with a radiance that
    illuminates the night
A beacon of hope
    that forever ignites
Lighten up my dear, lighten up

Sing a brand new song

Sometimes, your mind may want to stray
    to a place far, far away
Where you can escape the surrounding noise
    also, quietly screaming, that inner voice
    and start anew, a different life
Yes, you can leave it all behind
    but this monkey mind will soon find
    another way to disturb that life
For running away is not the tool
    to solve the problems you face
    or find the peace you want to embrace
So, stay, my dear
    but you can still move on
As your true guide
    let your heart carry on
    with the wings of courage
May you soar to the sky
    where you truly belong
And let your soul sing
    a brand-new song

You are enough

I am not good enough, smart enough
    tall enough, slim enough, lucky enough
These thoughts are not your self-judgments
    but this world's constant projections
Which often keep telling you that
    you must be more, do more
    achieve more, just something more
Making you look for outside validation
    from others wanting some appreciation
But let me remind you
    that you are already enough
Your worth is not defined
    by the standards of this world
You are not defined by your looks
    your achievement or possessions
You are not a product of this society
    but a unique and priceless creation
So, when those voices of doubt arise
    when the weight of expectations
    try to weigh you down, just remember
To feed yourself some self-love
    to give yourself a pat on the back
    with the soft touch of your hands
    even if they are wrinkled
Give your own self a smile
    in that moment even if it feels forced
Marvel at the spark in your eyes
    even if you see dark circles

Feel the blooming love in your heart
        even if there is still some pain not dissolved
Soak in the stillness of your being
        where none of this matters
        where you can simply be
        in the presence of your own magnificence
Stay there as long as you want
        and when you emerge back
Do keep reminding yourself
        again and again that
"I am enough, I am peace, I am joy
        I am love; I am all that there is
        I am this universe itself"
        and with this knowledge
        now go forth and conquer the world
With your light shining bright
        as a beacon of inspiration
        for all those who doubt
        their own worthiness
You are enough, my dear, more than enough
        a living reminder that we all are enough

Feel to heal

There will be times when perhaps
       nothing will make sense to you
No matter what you do
       your mind will overpower you
These moments may be brief
       or seem stretched to infinity
The weight of the world may
       make you feel unworthy
You may judge your own self
       and question why
       all your wisdom left
You will try to come out
       of this muggy place
       sooner and faster but
       the more you try, the more you feel
       trapped in it
So, when that happens, remember
       not to run away from it
       or judge yourself for it
       or try to fight it
       or seek a way to escape it
As sometimes the only way
       out is to face it with grace
It's not a such a big deal
       but it's time for you to feel
       that pain and let it heal
       like the mud around the lotus
       like the shadows on the moon

your pain will turn into a beautiful boon
For time is a teacher
    a messenger from above
And, if you will listen closely,
    in it you'll hear the call of love

Darkness can be a friend

Darkness has its own purpose
    it's a time to let go and rest
As the sun sets
    and night spreads its blanket
We sleep to feel rejuvenated
For without this calming darkness
    and the canopy of the moon and stars
    how would we ever sleep and be rested?
The soil in which we plant our seeds
    is often dark, damp, and cold
But from that space of shadows
    new life grows, which is
    a sight both tender and bold
A baby grows in the darkness of
    a mother's womb
    where there is total comfort
    and stories of creation untold
So, when you feel your
    light has somewhat dimmed
Just relax, don't worry
    don't judge yourself
Just know that darkness can be a friend
    a place to re-energize and mend
Just know that soon
    you will emerge back stronger
    with your light shining brighter

Strength in vulnerability

It's okay to let your guard down
    take off your cape
    cry your heart out
No need to cover your tears
    or hide your pain
    and feel ashamed of your fears
    from the people around you
It's okay to let them see
    don't worry about what they may think
You may be surprised at
    how compassionate some can be
    and you don't need to know
    the cause of your pain
It's okay to let it be
    whatever it is
Like a passing cloud in the sky
    your pain will burst
    and rain will fall
Then the sun will come
    and a rainbow will be formed
Through experience, you know
    that pain comes like raindrops
So, take off your cape
    let your guard down
    and let it drench you
For nothing is going to stay
    longer than the dewdrops

What if, I wonder

What if you could live without
    all your fears?
Letting go of all that matters
    to you like tears?
What if you could start anew
    not knowing at all what to do?
What if you could rejoice in
    all that comes with loneliness
    and see it as a time of
    self-reflection and stillness?
What if this was the defining
    moment of your life
    taking you on a journey
    free from strife?
What if you were to lose everything
    and gain nothing but a new beginning?
What if, beyond the darkness, light awaits
    where all your limiting beliefs will dissipate?
What if these questions inspire you
    to live each day with a new breakthrough?
What if, I wonder!

Living in the now

Gone is the past, forever changed
    no longer as it was nor could be rearranged
Now it resides in the present, a new moment
    no longer the usual familiarity
    but it holds the seeds of new possibility
Soon we embrace what is in the now
    letting go of why, what, and how
Happiness meets us in that very moment
    for it resides forever in the present
Fruits of future may look enticing
    but only in the present can we
    sow their seeds and samplings
Living in the now is also the key
    to the treasure of our own being
So, let what's gone be gone
    let future be where it belongs
    and let us live in the here and now
    where happiness awaits with its songs

Meaningful living

Life is as long as our breath
    as short as our breath can be
One breath, we're alive and well
    next, our soul can be out and free
In this life, we play many roles
    mom, sister, father
    teacher, brother, and friend
But when our breath doesn't return
    all these come to an end
Journey ahead is all by oneself
    it continues, it doesn't end
Where do we go?
What do we become
    when we leave this Earthly place?
Who will remember us and miss us
    when we are no longer face to face?
These questions arise
    in my mind's space
Not finding the answers
    I give myself some grace
Silence whispers and says,
    make sure you live
    a life that's meaningful
    full of love, compassion
    service and making it purposeful

So that when your time here is completed
    your life on Earth is truly celebrated
    and the journey ahead is fully guided
    making it a path that is all the way lighted

Let go of the sandcastles

Let it go....
How long can you hold on to the sandcastles?
How long can you hold so tight
    to things that will soon be out of sight?
How long can you remain trapped in the bubble?
Just let it go and feel the fall
    embrace the ride
It can't get any worse than this
You may fall, but you will eventually rise
    open your palm and let it be
    set yourself and your spirit free
    open your eyes and see the light
    the darkness has already taken flight
The bright warm sun
    the moonlit night and the starry sky
    are all waiting for you
    on the other side
Letting go is not defeat
    but a courageous act and
    a chance to greet
    your new life
    on the other side
So, let it go

Resilient hope

Crushed and shattered
    yet hope still lingers on
Opposing values intertwine
    as the life cycle goes on

Treasure the divine guide

In times when clarity eludes
    and doubts and fears abound
When all you want is to escape
    and disappear without a sound
It's in these moments, so obscure
    that those who love you true
    can see the strength within you
    and help you see it, too
They believe in you
    when your own faith seems
    to have left you
With little said and much conveyed
    their sincerity and love, so pure
    can make you smile through your tears
    and help you to endure
For they remind you of your own worth
    and all that you can face
Their support helps you
    find your own safe place
These precious few in your life
    are a treasure, rare and dear
Though you may not know them yet
    but when you find yourself in need
They'll come to you at just the right time
    and bring to you exactly what you need

All you may do is pray
    pray through your sobs
    pray asking for help
    even if your faith seems shaken
For the divine will guide your way
    and send you what you truly need

Just be a seeker

Formless may appear in any way
    and in any form
    a human, a book, a blog
    a talk, a sign, a song
Endless are the ways it appears
    but only one way to recognize it
That way is through your own heart
You will know when it
    resonates within you
    seems just right to you
For when you pray with
    heart so full and true
You will find the answers you seek
    and will know just what to do
When you feel it inside you
    go all in, deeper into it
Listen to its voice
    and shut out all other noises
You may need to listen
    to your own fears first
It may seem scary
    as you begin this search
But don't distract yourself
    with anything or anyone else

Do your best to stay there, pray
	soon you will find an opening
	you will hear a voice
	you will feel a presence
	and you will find yourself in that
	moment. Pray!!

Garden hacks

Sow the seed, nurture the plant
    and watch it grow into a strong tree
Witness the buds as they unfurl
    a testament to nature's swirl
But know that the fruit they bear
    may not be yours alone to share
After years of toil and dedication
    which lead to bountiful creation
You may never taste how it feels
    the nectar that brings joy and heals
Be dispassionate and rejoice
    in the happiness of others
    who are enjoying the fruit
    of your long, tireless
    passionate and selfless labor
After all, you are just a gardener
Nothing here belongs to you really
So, do what you can
    to the best you can
    and then let it go
Seeds, plants, trees, fruit
    are all just an illusion anyway!!

For seasons beyond seasons

Dust off the gone by, let it fly away
Make room for what's to come in a new way
Autumn's here, bringing with it
    a colorful feast
    falling leaves
    crisp air
    longer nights
A change with so much beauty in it
    and soon the trees will look barren
But does that mean they are broken
    or is it over or is it lost
    or is it just a rest period
    a time to prepare for the newness?
New leaves, new flowers
    freshness all around
    spring for sure follows
    after winter is over
    it's the law of nature
Each stage has its own beauty
    its own learning, its own lessons
Trees lose their leaves but don't despair
    for they know new growth will soon be there
Leaves never cry as they fall
    for they know that life awaits
    on the other side
    it continues, it never stops
A pause is just a breather
    it's for recovering, refocusing

Life continues unstoppable
        no matter what the season
        and being a witness to all
        changes in and around us
        bring us to a state of dispassion
        where there is no entanglement
        no attachments, no expectations
Living in the moment
        moment to moment
        here and now
        living fully in whatever phase
        we may be in
        brings a smile from deep within
        and you merge in the trees
        in the flowers, in the sunshine
        yet you don't and life continues!!!

The eternal essence

Like the shimmering dewdrops
    in the early morning light
Like the sweet fragrance of earth
    after the first rain
Like the refreshing cool breeze
    after a scorching summer day
Like the tender petals of a rose in full bloom
Once, we, too, were pure and unblemished
    filled with hope and boundless possibilities
    our eyes, sparkling with the fire
    of unbridled dreams
    our hearts full of the promise of love
When anything was a possibility
When imagination was still so young
When we were like those dewdrops
    like that fragrance
    like that cool breeze
    like those delicate rose petals
What happened to us?
As we look back and realize
    how time has flown since then
So much has happened
    so much has changed
Yet deep within our souls, we know
    we are still the same, we still feel the same

So, let the memory of those precious moments
    remind us of who we truly are
    and inspire us to keep dreaming
    to keep believing and to keep moving

Let your love reign

It creeps in quietly
 pretends to be righteous, yet
It's not pleased easily
Sometimes, it claims self-respect
 other times, it commands authority
 or a higher stance and says,
 "I know better, I am older, wiser
 I am in a better position than you
 so, you better just do what I say"
When blown out of proportion
 it causes great pain
 arguments arise
 hearts are strained
 communication breaks
 mind is in a mess
 blame and victimhood
 create more distress
When this game is at play
 don't feel guilty or ashamed
 don't judge yourself or others
 or play the blame game
Step back, become aware
 and take your time
 to connect back within
 until you feel sublime
Then reach out
 from a place of belonging

Speak your truth
    without expecting understanding
Do what needs to be done
    say what must be said
Give others time to process it
    in their own time and way
Watch out for this game
    again and again
Stay conscious and aware
And let your love reign

In you I trust

Endings and beginnings
    beginnings and endings
    too many too quickly
As life's seasons are changing
    everything seems to be shifting
It seems I am in the endless cycle
    of moving on and then restarting
    in the wink of my eyes
    it's happening
In this constant flux
    let me be that being who is unwavering
Whatever comes and goes
    let me be the one who is witnessing
Just like I watch the leaves falling
    and patiently wait for the new sprouting
    let me find myself being firm in my standing
    and only the best will eventually be happening
This be my strong belief, so to you I am praying
    let me rely on your grace, so in you I am trusting
No matter what the endings and what the beginnings!!!

SECTION 5:

Through time's trace

An endless wait

I waited and waited
    for the storms to pass
    for our lives to return to normal
    just the way it was supposed to be
    just the way we wanted it to be
But the wait was long and tiring
    no sign of hope, no silver lining
The waves crashed down on us hard
    leaving us alone and scarred
    our world crumbled
    hearts were broken
    lives were shattered
    words unspoken
We drifted apart to separate islands
    where pain and isolation were
    the only companions
    days, months, and years were
    in constant commotion
    time passed in slow motion
My courage struggled to overcome the darkness
    multiple times I crashed feeling the brokenness
But then I survived getting back the calmness
    and the wait flickered igniting the hopefulness

My life continued to feel like an endless wait
        for a world of love with a better fate
        in which storms were weathered
        hearts were united
        lives were nurtured
        and words were understood

Circle of life

Everything that starts eventually ends
    and when it does, again it begins
    the cycle goes on
    as time flows on
But what lies beyond this circle
    out of this loop remaining eternal
Is my life really of any worth
    in this endless chain of death and birth
I wonder as I witness yet another ending
    and wait for a new form to start breathing
But until the time the answer is found
    in life's circle forever I am bound
Let me remain true to my seeking
    as the secrets get ready for revealing

Cutting through the darkness

Her needs may have been few
    but her heart was boundless and true
Love was all that she ever wanted
    but, in this wanting, her own self
    she almost abandoned
    and then slipped back
    into a corner of the house
    like an old painting
    collecting dust in the garage
    like a forgotten sock
    laying in a drawer unopened
She felt not seen, not wanted
    lost in the shadows of her mind
Her laughter vanished, not to be found
    her love for life got suffocated
    and she became someone she
    herself couldn't comprehend
She put up thick curtains
    to avoid the sun's rays so bright
But she had forgotten
    that she herself was the light
    and darkness couldn't hide her
    for too long
Also, the resilience inside her
    was too strong
So, she emerged back
    following her own track
    slowly but surely

gradually but happily
one beam at a time
one day at a time
Bright and beautiful
strong and purposeful
Now she was awakened
forever more determined
To brighten her own light
to cut through any night
Illuminating the world
as she rises to a new height

Transition to transformation

For years, she thought she was a vine
    and needed a tree for her survival
That's all she had lived like
    there was no other way
It shook her from the core
    she howled for days
When a storm shook everything
    and she fell flat on the ground
Despair and hopelessness consumed her
    and darkness enveloped her all around
Not knowing what to do
    she waited for the Earth to swallow her
"My time here has come to an end"
    she thought, but a little
    desire to live was still inside her
She stayed there still in the hope
    that the tree would eventually pick her
    and the bad dream-like phase would
    be forever behind her
Though this never happened
    she realized her breath was still with her
    she didn't wither away like a vine
    her leaves stayed green and she
    relied on courage which she didn't
    even know was inside her
So, gradually she stood up
    still trembling in fear
    thinking maybe one last time

she could hold on to the tree
and say a proper goodbye
closure was important for her
The distance between them had widened
since the time she had fallen
There was no way she could cover it
so, she failed to lean upon it
and, to her surprise,
She realized something quite profound
that she was standing on her own solid ground
though she was trembling with fear
thinking a fall was again almost near
But patiently she waited
just a little more time
She froze in joyful disbelief
as slowly slipped away the time
and she kept standing
So, she started believing
that she wasn't a vine after all
but a tree herself standing tall
She looked towards the sky
and prayed, "Oh Lord,
please make my roots stronger
let my branches grow wider
so I can take under my wings
anyone who can use my shelter"

Now she stood tall and humble
        though wind of fear still crept in
        feeling like a storm from time to time
But now she knew that she was enough
        that she would continue to thrive
        and during all changing weathers
        she will be hopeful that
        she is a tree strong enough

Weathering the storm

It wasn't a huge incident
It wasn't so tiny either
But my heart was tender
It got rubbed on
      and now it's very huge
      with emotions that overflow
It feels like volcano that's
      ready to erupt and blow
But I'll weather this storm inside
      and find a way to rise above
For though pain is hard to hide
      I'll find a way to heal

Dropping causality

What is it that hurts so bad that sometimes
    it's an effort even to breathe?
Shattered dreams and hopes
    broken expectations, saddened hearts
    or pain of lost love and trust?
Yet, amidst the darkness and despair,
    what is it that keeps us hopeful?
Self-confidence, divine love
    our own resilience
    faith beyond ourselves
    or is it just our nature
    to keep moving on?
No matter what comes our way
    the cycle of life keeps going on

Are you watching

Someday, I may burst like a cloud
    for now, I am keeping it all inside
Yes, I am strong and I won't give up
    but sometimes I feel I've had enough
    and I long for a little time to unwind
Tides will change, clouds will lift
    but, for now, I am okay with the fog
I am just looking for a little assurance
    that you see the water rising to my shoulders
Are you really watching
    so that I'll keep moving forward
    taking it one day at a time
    trusting the brighter skies are ahead
    and holding on to the hope
    that one day I won't feel
    like I'm drowning anymore?

Grateful heart restored

All is well within me
    and it feels like I am myself again
The sun shines bright as usual
    and clear blue sky is seen again
The songs in my heart are humming
    and I have no choice but to be smiling
    with a resolve to be fully living
    and embracing each moment
    with a sense of knowing
I am grateful for the wonderful friends
    who sent me love and blessings
    who reminded me of hope and strength
    during those intense passing moments
    those moments came and went
But I stand here stronger and wiser
    wishing you all a life much happier
    from a grateful heart that
    has been restored once again

When footing is not firm

Nothing is broken nor needs fixing
    it is what it is
When you ask me, "What happened?"
Know that it's like asking
    how much hair I have on my head
    or how many stars are in the sky
Perhaps someone can count these two
    but I can't answer this question
    as I haven't figured it out myself, yet
Just know that it is a happening
    beyond our control
You don't need to sympathize or
    do anything at all
Just meet me in my now, if possible
    or please leave me alone
    till you can let go of the image
    you had about my life
Just because my life
    doesn't fit your frame
    doesn't mean you now have
    the right to preach to me
    or gossip behind my back
There is enough turbulence already
    and my footing is not firm completely
So, let's just keep it easy
    let's just let it flow
I am letting the winds carry me forward
I am just going with the flow

Not knowing where I am heading to
        but move I must so life can go on
Come walk with me if you can

Blank space

"How do you write blankness in words?"
I am thinking, flying from SFO to Charlotte
    as I feel nothing
    nothing, like an empty space
    like the blank canvas
All that once seemed like
    my life
    has drifted away
I feel I am like the soft clay
    ready to be shaped and molded
    into something new
What colors, expressions
    divinity will give now
    to discover part of myself
    yet unshown
A journey that will unfold
    in moment unknown

Unfazed

"What happened," they asked with concern
    curiosity and judgment in their voices
Their faces showed shock, as if they learned
    something that left them with difficult choices
When I replied, "It's just a happening"
    their expressions turned into a puzzle
    suddenly, I was a culprit in their silent noises
So, let them judge and gossip as they please
    for my heart is pure and my intentions are true
Their opinions cannot diminish my inner peace
    or change the fact that I am still me
    through and through

In the moment connections

They asked me, "Where have you been?"
And I replied, "I am here now"
But the look on their faces
    was wanting to see
    my previous version
    which was perhaps more
    familiar and known to them
They were wanting
    to know the past
    what had happened
    and what was really going on
I was hoping for them
    to be fully present
    to meet me
    in this new moment
With no questions
    guesses and judgments
What if we could all
    meet each other like this?
From moment to moment
    fresh and blank like new canvases?
With no baggage, no expectation
    and no hesitation
Wouldn't it be a better way
    and a happier us?

Imagine a world where
    we could all shed our past
    and embrace each other
    in the present
With open hearts, open minds
    and open arms
A world where we could
    truly see each other
    and connect on a deeper
    more authentic level

Through time's trace

Time gone by
    and yet she stands tall
Some silver in her hair
    and wrinkles on her face
A body that brought life
    into this world
Years of work done
    through those tireless hands
Feet that moved in
    the direction of love alone
Nurturing her family
    and supporting her community
    with dedication, zeal, and patience
A tale of storms she weathered
    hidden under those eye bags
    and faced obstacles that
    only few could overcome
She stands now
    all by herself
Looking around at
    everything that's gone by
At all that's been created
    with her as a background
Seeds she planted have
    grown into trees
Fruits that ripened
    for others to seize
Who are blissfully

unaware of the toil
she went through
and though time may
have left its trace
Her spirit shines
with an enduring grace

For the first time in forever

"Listen to your own inner voice," they said
"Let your intuition guide your way"
But when I listened, they screamed and objected
    I should conform and deflect, they demanded
    and do only what their opinions say
But I took the leap against their noise
    and for the first time in a long time
I followed my inner voice's way
    and it felt so right day after day
    a freedom filled me up all the way
I was no more holding on to
    anything that didn't want to stay
    or trying to fix it and hoping
    that it didn't slip away
I moved from what I didn't want
    to what I truly wanted
    and then one fine day
I dropped both wanted and unwanted
    as I looked towards the sky
    with my arms wide open and said
"Do what you think is best for us all"
    and the voice within me started being
    louder and clearer every day
    I just followed it in every possible way
I stopped asking questions and
    guidance itself started coming my way

Noises of others long faded away
    and I started finding myself more each day
The clear, crisp, soft, and sweet voice
    started singing in my ears along the way

Lonely night towards the light

Falling raindrops from the sky
    on a dark, cold, winter night
I stand here surrounded by emptiness
    wondering where all those went
    whom this house gave warmth and comfort
What happened to all those promises
    of being there for each other and not desert
But now no one is in this space
    leaving the heart to bear
    the weight of loneliness
    as warm tears stream down my face
But deep within flickers a flame every day
    of hope and belief that
    this, too, shall soon pass
    and only the best will come my way
With chanting and prayers
    I seek comfort in the divine
As I fall asleep, night after night
    hoping to get guided towards the light

Your life awaits, go meet it

Amidst the shifting tides of life
    and the people who come and go
It's not about you, my friend
    it never was, don't you know?
Everyone is trying to
    fill their own void
Something they feel they lack
    and haven't figured it out yet
So, they keep going forward and back
    from person to person
    party to party, place to place
But you don't need to compare yourself
    with their forever changing space
Because it's not about you at all
    you were solid
    you were focused
    you were committed
    you did all you could have done
    you waited patiently
    you allowed them space
    to grow and to be free
Now you are free
    and it's time to focus on yourself
    your growth
    your happiness
    your freedom
    your heart
    your dreams

Let them continue their search
      of whatever they are seeking
      their life is not your concern
Your life is waiting, go meet it
      and live it like you
      have never lived before

Looking for a new start

In the middle of the night
I sit and ponder as to
    what I am doing
    all alone in this house
    which is spacious and beautiful
My needs are small, and I am dutiful
But my dreams are big and purposeful
    and in the balance only I am joyful
Though I still feel laughter's absence
    as I wait for a miracle to unfold
I fear that my life will remain
    a story which was never told
As days go on one after another
    I wish for more, something better
Something like the innocent laughter
    being surrounded by fullness thereafter
To make each day like a new start
    finding passion again in my heart
So, I hold on to hope in the unseen
    letting time bring a change in the scene

This shall also pass

You gave it your all, you truly did
    you took every chance you could
You tried and tried, again and again
    waited patiently, with hope within
You worked hard
    gave it your hundred percent
Not quitting but letting it go
    that's how it was meant
    if it didn't return
    if it didn't work out
    if it didn't appreciate
    if it didn't go well
Then it wasn't meant to be
    wasn't worth your time
    wasn't worth your wait
There is nothing more for you to do
    just letting life start healing you
I know it still hurts; I know it's tough
    it brings you down, making it rough
But have faith this shall also pass
    as everything here must come to pass
You are going to be okay; it will get better
    With some time more, with some steps later
You will stop hurting, you will start healing
    you will stop waiting, you will have a new beginning

Learning unlearning

"Who am I?"
I have asked myself a thousand times
    in the silence of dark lonely nights
    sitting awake unable to sleep
    no roles to fill a vacuum deep
What am I doing here
    listening for some answers to appear
Night after night on the same track
    silence alone is what echoes back
Then, with courage, I shed away
    layers of everything I thought I was
    unlearning all I had learnt every day
    questioning what my true purpose was
I look back at the time slipped away
    when I was busy playing wholeheartedly
    all those roles which now drifted away
    like changing seasons swiftly gone by
Or, perhaps, I walked towards myself more
    to let my inner self show for evermore
My eyes opened to a new world within
    mine to explore without others perception
I am getting used to this new way
    letting the inquiry deepen every day
Who am I now?
Who will I want to be going forward?
I am in no rush to find all the answers
    as this inquiry itself is my navigator

I am okay for the first time ever
    not needing to figure it all out whatsoever
I realize it's a process, a lifelong journey
    of learning and unlearning without any hurry
In moments here and there by myself
    I feel I am on the brink of finding myself

Flight of the caged bird

A bird in the cage
    remains imprisoned
    even if the cage is of gold
    gold doesn't make it happy
Yes, it's safe from the predators
    it's fed without having to look for food
    it's not affected by the outside environment
But what use is this kind of life
    where there is no freedom, no adventure?
Can it ever have the feeling of returning to nest
    after a long day flying miles away from home
    looking for food, along with many more birds
    the clouds, the sun, the earth
    the wind, the water, the challenge
    the fear, the fun, and being
    with the beauty that lies
    outside of its prison, its wings clipped
    unable to make any decision?
I look at the bird in the cage
    I see the life in its eyes
    and I feel the pain it feels
The irony is that even if you set it free
    it won't go anywhere
    as it has never seen the world out there
It has never known how to
    live under the open skies
With its pretty colors and soft feathers
    it has been in the cage as far as it remembers

I look at the bird again, and
    it keenly looks back at me
    as if reading my mind
    and all my thoughts about it
It flies to me and sits on my shoulder
    as if wanting to say, "Don't worry about me
    I am okay, I am perfectly fine
    I am loved, and, yes, the freedom is very precious
    but trust me, I do feel free
I may be locked up in sight
    but my thoughts and dreams can take flight
In my mind, I can soar and explore
    and be free as I've always been before"
The bird in the cage, though little
    yet larger than life itself
It made me wonder as to what
    the true meaning of freedom is?
Is it only a condition of being unconfined
    or also a state of mind, a feeling within?
For in the end, it's not about our chains
    or the cages that hold us in our pain
It's about our spirit, our will to do
    and this freedom lives in me and you
So, let us break free and take a flight
    giving it our all, with all our might

Break free

I break free from every chain
    feeling a sense of freedom again
I set myself and all of you free
    free to be who we're meant to be
No longer trapped in boxes tight
    or shackled by the stories we write
We're free to be the voice of humanity
    writing songs of peace and unity
To live in the space of amazingness
    and feel with all, a sense of belongingness

On the wings of faith

My mind is my only cage
    other than that, I am free
When it dissolves, its bliss
    when it stands tall, it's misery
I am learning to be a witness
    to this fall and the rise
Without craving bliss
    or running away from misery
Do I succeed?
    sometimes yes and others no
But one thing remains constant
    one thing that walks me
    through it all
    is my faith in the divine
That it is always there for me
    that it doesn't matter how I feel
As every time it pulls me out
    and shows me that
    I am more than all this
No matter how many times I fall
    it helps me rise above this
It becomes my guiding light
    in the darkness of ignorance
When my mind gets muddy
    it washes it off
    just with its memory
I feel blessed to have this faith
    in my heart

That keeps me going
    when the path is hard
I pray that my faith remains
    strong and deep
No matter how slippery
    the path may be
For with it
    I can walk, I can crawl, run, or fly
    and find the strength to soar up high

Bruting the diamond

A storm began to brew
I tried holding it down
    hoping it would subdue
    but it fought and struggled
    trying to disrupt everything
I was almost getting tired
    holding it down
It has been a real struggle
My strength tested in the hustle
Just now I see a little hope
    a little release
Calm is slowly setting in
    witness mode is being restored
The thunder of shock and emotions is
    giving way to the sound of peace
I am allowing myself to stay
    present with every emotion
    and letting it play itself out
Not being hard on myself
    and not expecting anyone else
    to understand the pain
    I am going through
The web of Maya, a tangled mess
    not easy to break through
But as the storm recedes
I will start seeing it for what it is
    and pick myself up piece by piece

I will emerge back stronger
      wiser and brighter
It was, perhaps, another phase
      of cutting, refining
      scrubbing, polishing
      the diamond that I am becoming

Home is where the heart is

A building is not a home, is it?
If not, then what is a home?
I wondered as I pulled out of
    the driveway of this house
    after dropping off my daughters
This house which used to be my home
    in which I spent a big part of my life
Is it the walls, floors, or ceiling
    that make a place feel like home
    or the memories, moments, and people
    that make it a sanctuary of our own?
In that humble abode that once was mine
    I nurtured my children and watched them grow
    I shared my joy, laughter, and tears
    and built a lifetime of memories to glow
But as I left from outside
    knowing the festivities unfolding inside
I realized that home isn't a place I left behind
    but a feeling that I carry inside myself
Home is a state of mind
    a place where we find comfort, peace, and love
It could be a moment, a person, or a place
    that makes us feel seen, cherished, and safe
How times change, I wondered
    as I found a cozy, comfortable spot within me
    happiness and peace flowing through me
In those moments, I felt totally at home

Home is certainly where I am present
         in totality, in unity, and in divinity
So, home could be a place, a moment in time
         or the entire time in one moment
Home sweet home

From ashes to diamond

It's not about them anymore
What they did or didn't do
It's about how I felt
    how it pierced my heart
    how it made me shrink
    how it made me feel small
    not enough, not loved
    barely able to stand tall
But then it's also about
    how I arose from the ashes
    the smoke still coming
    the fire still burning
Clear, cool, crisp breeze
    flowing into my breath
Bringing me some peace
    one breath at a time
I regained my strength
    one step at a time
I maintained my courage
For in the end
    it wasn't about them
It was about
    what happened to me
    and what emerged from within me
    a precious gem
The fire was excruciating
    but it was the only way
    to reveal that

I was not a stone
but a diamond meant to
sparkle and shine alone
Now it's about my light
shining bright
Lighting up the world
with a dazzling sight
one house at a time
one person at a time
and it's my promise to myself
To keep igniting many more lights
to carve out many more diamonds
For it's not about the fire that blazed
but what emerged from the flames, unfazed

Director's cut

I once thought you were to be blamed
    for all my misery and my pain
Up until the curtain was raised
    a replay of everything was staged
For me to see clearly
    that you were not there
    to begin with
There was no other, just me
Then who did what to me?
If I was all there was,
    then I did all this
    to myself?
Oh Good Lord
I can finally start to see
    what a big fool I have been
But now as I see with clear sight
    I alone must take the flight
To heal my wounds and ease my mind
    and leave the blame and pain behind
I have all it takes to change my fate
    and live a life that's truly great

I am with you

Looking for an opening, a sign
    a path unfolding under my feet
    in search of a glimmer
    a spark to reignite
    a beacon of hope to
    guide me through the night
Yearning for wings to soar high
    a gentle hand tapping on my shoulder
A graceful voice saying, "I am with you
    go on, carry on, my dear
No matter what comes your way
    take a moment to relax
    take a little longer to rest fully
It's okay to let your guard down
    you cannot be strong all the time
Let your tears roll
    then wipe your face
    smile and go do what you need to do
Just remember, I am with you
    you are never alone, my dear
    I am always right by you"

Love is the only song

I became anxious
Time felt like sand slipping
     through my hands
My mind became confused
     asking whether to continue or discontinue
     as it seemed too hard
     too time-consuming
     too little time for myself
     and I thought, "When will I go
     to those far-off places calling me?"
Something in me was wanting to go
     to explore the world, seek new adventures
     to get a fresh breath of life
     to find a deeper purpose of my life
Amidst this confusion
     in a moment of surrender
I released this burden and
     let go of the weight
My mind felt clear and
     something got lifted off my heart
I looked up at the clear blue sky
     and prayed, "Oh universe, please guide me
     show me the way towards
     my role in this world
     bring me clarity and flow through me
     as my best version of me"
Looking back, I realize
     since then, my life shifted and changed

Purposeful connections and
        deeper conversations emerged
Love started flowing from every direction
No rush in my mind and patience blossomed
Moment by moment, living life
        doing what needs to be done
I became a vessel, a hollow flute
        an instrument of the divine
No matter what music played through me
        love was the only song that mattered

.

From senses to beingness

As one more day slowly fades into the night
    and darkness envelops everything in sight
She sits in her bed, comfortable and warm
    gazing out of the window
    at the world's glowing charm
The dark wilderness lay before her eyes
    with city lights twinkling in the backdrop high
A little kitten nestled by her side
    in deep slumber, all it's worries aside
She just sits there, lost in her own thoughts
    neither fully aware, nor quite lost
Her eyes take in the beauty of scene
    her mind adrift, like a river serene
She is neither asleep nor really awake
    for she's attuned to the beingness
    the essence of all that exists
    in a state of pure awareness
She feels as if nothing else is around her
    though she can still see, touch, and smell
    everything that is in the room with her
Outside, the rain falls, distant sounds
    echo here and there
But inside, stillness spreads from within her
    to outside everywhere
As she basks in this amazingness
    a smile shines from within
And she just sits there
    in the purest form of beingness

Beyond the confines of duality

I am but a work in progress
    neither perfect nor imperfect, I confess
Yet a wise person once told me that
    I am something beyond the perception
I often wonder
    what could it mean to be in that place
    to reside in equanimity
    like the never-ending space
    to be free from life's constant change
Though in fleeing moments
    I have known of peace and calm
    briefly shown here and there
But to reside there permanently
    I wonder how far that journey still is
But nonetheless I shall strive
    with heart and soul
To reach that state
    is my goal
To be in equanimity all the time
    to transcend the opposites, the sublime
    to live beyond the confines of duality
    and bask in the infinite's eternal reality

The assurance of presence

In the depth of despair
    when darkness seemed to reign
A gentle voice whispered
    and lifted me from pain
    no questions asked
    no explanation required
    no words were needed
Just the assurance of presence
    and the warmth of love provided
"Know that you are not alone"
"I am with you"
    the power of these few words
    resonated deep in my soul
    and lifted me higher
    towards a brighter goal
    and just like that abundance, love
    and light filled me up
    making me complete and whole

Path of joy

It was a fleeting moment when time stood still
    as I sought guidance for a void to fill
Sharing with my teacher what phase
    my life was going through
In his gaze, it felt like the whole
    universe was shown through
    and with a voice of compassion
He spoke true, "I am with you,
    and you have lots of work to do"
    twice he said so
Every day since then
    a newfound joy I feel
    as my desires, worries, ambitions unseal
    leading me to a place
    guided by my soul
    wherein lies everything
    a wondrous whole
With a smile from ear to ear
I exclaim, "That's it, I've got it all"
As my soul inflames in realization
    that he is with me always
    leading me to the path of joy
    every single day

Expanding horizons

The sunshine beams so bright
    on this glorious day, full of light
Spring colors dance before my eyes
    as chirping birds fly to the sky
My heart is full of gratitude
    for this moment of peaceful solitude
After weeks of chaos and hustle
    for all challenges and the struggle
    that comes my way and shows
    me my strength every day
    deepening my faith and love
    which no one can ever take away
For all those sent my way
    crossing paths with me each day
With every moment that passes by
    my horizons expand as I soar high
In this ever-changing world
    I find my own way, day by day

Union

You and me both
disappeared, dissolved
What remains is what is

It is what it is

Perhaps there are mountains to be climbed
    gardens to enjoy and oceans to be explored
    people to meet and places to be lived
But I am so content being where I am
    knowing what I know, doing what I do
There is no grip of desires or dreams
    of doing something big, of people and places
    or changing the world, creating new spaces
Contentment, like a subtle mantra, now resides
    in me and me in it
Perhaps I'm deemed lazy by some
    or lacking ambition to overcome
But in this contentment, I find my rest
    and in this state, I feel truly blessed
    at peace, in abundance
    in gratitude, in bliss
Who knows, maybe this is what it is

Home is where ego is done

To me, home is not just a place
But a state of being also
Where you and I meet
	like rivers merging into
	the ocean, becoming one
Every moment and every place
	can feel like home
Whenever the ego is done
May this feeling of oneness
	and belonging never fade
	and may I always reside
In the ocean of self, unafraid

An eternal union

For years, I wandered aimlessly
    seeking you out in vain
Longed for a chance
    to meet you
    to ease my heart's deep pain
    and then I stopped looking
    as I turned within
There to my surprise
    I found you patiently waiting
    in the depths of
    my own sweet being
You were always within
    here and everywhere
Now our union is eternal
    and I feel your presence
    all around and everywhere

Exploring uncharted shores

There is a wave in my heart
It surges beyond the known boundaries
    guiding me towards uncharted shores
    to explore the depth of my inner core
With each surge, I discover more
    and with every retreat, I soar

A spontaneous celebration

A cool breeze whispers through the trees
    in the moonlit sky, my heart feels so free
The warmth of food fills my soul
    and takes me back in time
    to happy days and childhood memories
As I revel in the beauty of this moment
    I find my mind fully in the present
My favorite dinner spot turns into
    a place for spontaneous celebration
For celebrations need no external reason
They arise from love and joy within
    and every moment is a gift
    to be cherished and lived fully herein

Roar

Hear me roar, for I am no longer hiding
My light shines bright, no longer dimming
For too long, I shrank and suffocated
Afraid to be seen, to be celebrated
But now I rise with newfound strength
My spirit soaring, no longer restricted
    and I bring with me so many more souls
    whose light was also kept dimmed
Together we rise, unbound and untamed
    bursting with a brilliance yet unclaimed

A dinner date

Today I took myself out for dinner
It was a special day
    just because I felt like it
It was like the newness of first love
    when you just can't wait
    to see your beloved
You blush, lost in your thoughts
    and giggle for no reason
The difference today was that
    I showered love on my own self
    and happiness spread from within
It was flowing from me to me
    and the whole world seems
    to have gotten drenched in it

Love is in the air

I look into her eyes and
    see the light of life
Her soft glowing skin
    and lovely warm smile
"You are beautiful," I say,
    "kind and happier everyday
How wonderful you are
    glowing and radiating
    divinity in you is manifesting"
She just smiles back at me
    with love and appreciation
Yes, I look at her every morning
    as I gaze into the mirror
She is no one but my own reflection
It has taken me some time
    to truly see
What it means
    to be in love with me
    to appreciate every inch, every cell
    to feel the freedom within so well
I am complete in my reflection
    a wonder, a perfection, a true connection
    and, as I look into the mirror each day,
    I see your creation now in a new way

Savoring life's simplicity

Basking in the warm embrace of the sun
    in the sanctuary of my own heaven
Sitting in the patio
    of my own restaurant
Savoring the delectable food
    my soul finds solace and serenity
    with a heart
    brimming with gratitude
    for this beautiful life
    gifted to me
I relish the simplicity
    of this moment
As if there is
    nowhere to go
    nothing to do
    no botherations
    no hesitations
    no expectations
And a big yes
    to the present moment
Feeling in this moment
    that I am enough
    in my own way
That I am here to spread
    joy, bliss, and peace
    to everyone around
    each and every day

Embracing the unknown

Not knowing how and what
    I step outside the bounds of reason
With faith as my guide
    I embrace the unknown
There is something there so sublime
    a presence deep inside
Beyond space and time
    like the vastness of endless sky
A sense of freedom
    that words can't describe
There is something just being in it
    to revel in the wonder of it
For in that present moment
    I am totally free
    and that is enough for me

Simply being

I sit and simply just be
    fully immersed in this moment
    here and now
    where all is well
    and everything is taken care of
It's a wonderful state of being
One where I feel
    both empty and full
Like a wave merging with the ocean
    and the ocean being the wave
    or, perhaps, it's something in between
A space where water is
    so calm and still
    that nothing really moves at all
In this stillness, I find expansion
    a sense of wholeness and completeness
    a fullness that goes beyond words
The silence is rich and profound
    and it speaks to me in ways
    that words cannot
It fills me up and
    I am content
    simply being here in
    this present moment

I am my own garden

I have learnt to be my own garden
    no matter how small
It's of my own hard work
    I have invested in it
    worked in and on it
I haven't stolen the soil
    from under another's feet
I have put myself as a seed
    under the ground
    dark lonely times
When I broke open
I was in such turmoil
    as I feared it was the end
But then the sprouts came
Soon I saw the daylight
    sun shining on me
    clouds showering me
    air caressing me
    and a sweet presence
    embracing me
It was all there even before
    but I couldn't realize it
    as fear had blocked my vision
I still get nervous sometimes
My heart beats faster
My mind starts running
But now my faith
    is well established

in the strength
of my roots
in the care of my creator
and I have learnt to bloom
in the oddest of circumstances
I am my own garden
adding beauty back to the universe

About the Author

Satinder Kaur is a transformational life coach, speaker, and writer who ignites inspiration wherever she goes. Her journey, marked by resilience, creativity, and profound spiritual awakening, serves as a beacon for those seeking personal growth and self-discovery.

Born and raised in the vibrant landscapes of India, Satinder is a multifaceted individual whose journey encompasses a rich tapestry of academic excellence, entrepreneurial spirit, and dynamic leadership.

From an early age, she displayed an innate talent for creativity, lending her voice to song and speeches, writing poetry, and being on stage all while extending a helping hand to those around her. She pursued degrees in arts and literature and later earned a master's in law, thus shaping her intellect and broadening her horizons in her homeland.

Venturing to the United States as a first-generation immigrant, Satinder embarked on a new chapter, where she further enriched her knowledge with a master's degree in international business practices from McGeorge School of Law in 1998.

Her professional journey was a testament to grit, determination, and resilience as she co-founded, owned, and managed two thriving businesses—a prestigious law firm and an award-winning Indian restaurant, which became a beloved staple in the community.

Yet it was a transformative encounter with spiritual luminary Sri Sri Ravi Shankar in 2007 that deeply altered Satinder's path. Embracing the teachings of ancient wisdom, the power of breath and meditation, she discovered profound inner peace and purpose, leading her to become an Art of Living facilitator in 2008. Since then, she has served as a beacon of empowerment, touching the lives of thousands with her wisdom and compassionate guidance.

A devoted mother to her two daughters, a certified Sri Sri yoga teacher, and a Lisa Nichols Certified Transformational Trainer and Speaker Advocate Coach, Satinder wears multiple hats with ease, dedication, and joy.

Through life's myriad challenges, she has remained steadfast in her commitment to personal evolution, leaning on her unshakable faith, boundless determination, and indomitable courage, transforming adversity into opportunities for personal growth and self-discovery, and inspiring countless individuals along the way. In every role she undertakes, Satinder radiates joy, compassion, and the unwavering belief in the limitless potential of the human spirit.

Made in the USA
Las Vegas, NV
23 November 2024

12480782R00121